A New True Book

EXPERIMENTS WITH HEAT

By Walter Oleksy

CHILDRENS PRESS ®

CHICAGO

Old Faithful, a geyser in
Yellowstone National Park

PHOTO CREDITS

Tony Freeman Photographs—4 (top), 7, 9, 11
(2 photos), 15, 21 (left), 25, 29 (2 photos), 30, 33
(2 photos), 40, 41, 42

Bob Glickman—23

Jerry Hennen—16

Image Finders:
© R. Flanagan—37

Journalism Services:
© Mark Gamba—10
© John Patsch—18, 27

NASA—Cover, 12, 45 (2 photos)

Nawrocki Stock Photo:
© Michael Brohm—2, 34
© Jim Whitmer—4 (bottom)
© Ken Love—13
© M & S Photo—39

John Forsberg—17, 21 (right), 22

*With appreciation to Dave Dannels,
science instructor,
Evanston Township High School,
Evanston, Illinois,
for consultation and experiments*

Library of Congress Cataloging-in-Publication Data

Oleksy, Walter G., 1930-
  Experiments with heat.

  (A New true book)
  Includes index.
  Summary: Scientific explanations and experiments
demonstrate the nature of heat, its sources, and how it
travels and affects matter.
  1. Heat—Juvenile literature. 2. Heat—Experiments—
Juvenile literature. [1. Heat—Experiments. 2. Experi-
ments] I. Title.
QC256.O57   1986   537   85-30860
ISBN 0-516-01277-0

TABLE OF CONTENTS

Solar hot-water panels (above) are used to heat some homes.
Heat is used to cook food, too.

HEAT

Heat warms us and our homes. It cooks the food we eat. It helps plants grow.

Heat is used in factories to make everything from bricks and glass to automobiles and TV sets.

Heat engines convert heat into energy for useful work. Examples of heat engines are compressors, steam or gas engines, turbines, jet and rocket engines.

Heat makes things move. It can cause a train engine to go or send a rocket soaring into outer space.

Most heat we use comes from the sun. Without it, all living things would die. The earth would become cold and dead, like the moon.

EXPERIMENT

Turn on a light bulb. Feel the heat from the side of the bulb? You're feeling radiant heat— radiation.

Feel the heat near the top. You're feeling convected heat— convection. It will feel warmer than it does from the sides.

WHAT IS HEAT?

Heat is a form of energy. Often, this energy is in the form of the motion of molecules.

Most of the things we see every day are made up of tiny particles called molecules. The smallest bit of any one thing is a molecule. A molecule of water is the tiniest bit of water.

EXPERIMENT

Rub your hands together. They begin to feel warm, don't they? You've generated heat because the motion of your hands is converted into motion of the molecules in your skin.

Molecules are in constant motion. The faster the molecules in an object move, the warmer the object becomes.

Heat is the energy that a body at a higher

Rowers turn their potential energy into kinetic energy.

temperature transfers to a body at a lower temperature with some loss of its total energy.

Total energy is made up of two parts: kinetic energy and potential energy.

Kinetic energy is the energy of motion. Potential energy is a thing's possible or stored-up energy.

Potential energy is positional energy. Anytime you have to do work or exert a force to move something to another position, you put potential, or stored-up, energy into it.

Experiment: When you pull a rubber band back (left), you store potential energy into it. When you let go, this potential energy becomes kinetic energy—the energy of motion.
Experiment: A book (right) has potential energy. When it falls, the motion of falling converts potential (stored-up) energy into kinetic (moving) energy.

Rockets carry the space shuttle into space.

Rockets work on this same principle. Stored potential energy in the rocket's fuel is converted into kinetic energy—energy of motion—that can blast the rocket into space.

Often, one form of energy can be converted easily into another. For

Windmills are used to generate electricity on this wind farm.

example, kinetic energy contained in rushing water, or even the wind, can be converted into electrical energy by a generator.

Nuclear energy can be used to warm water to make high-pressure steam, which can run a generator to make electrical power.

SOURCES OF HEAT

Almost all the heat we use comes from the sun, either directly or indirectly. It comes to us directly by shining on us, to give us heat and light.

We get the sun's heat indirectly from coal, wood, oil, and gas, which all contain energy from the sun. They are the fossil fuels, remains of ancient plants and animals that

The sun warms the earth and makes life on earth possible.

got their energy from the sun.

Heat also comes from other sources. The interior of the earth is very hot. Examples are lava boiling inside volcanoes and steam from geysers. The earth's interior heat isn't used much today. Someday, scientists may learn how to use it better.

Heat also is produced when atoms are broken down. Heat and energy are created that way in nuclear power plants.

Nuclear power plant

EXPERIMENT

Friction, the rubbing of one object against another, creates heat. Scouts learn to start a fire using a bow and drill to create friction.

A back-and-forth "sawing" motion with the bow causes the drill bit to spin quickly. As the scout leans harder on the drill it causes more friction creating more heat. Soon smoke rises from the block of wood. The smoke indicates a spark. A spark indicates fire.

These are primary sources of heat, but there are other ways of creating heat. Friction can create heat.

When a race car zips
off in a race, its tires
begin to spin on the
pavement. They "burn
rubber."

The energy to produce this heat comes from the kinetic energy of the car's motion.

Remember what you learned about kinetic energy? When you exert a force or make an object move, you can convert or change one form of energy into another. You can convert kinetic or chemical energy into heat.

HOW HEAT TRAVELS

Let's look at two fundamental laws of nature. One is that everything wants to become chaotic or disorganized.

The other law is that everything wants to go to its lowest energy level.

All objects want to cool off, to get to their lowest energy level. They will give up their heat in order to give up their energy.

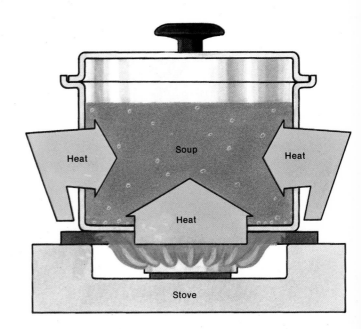

Irons are built to give off heat.

Warm objects will give off their heat to cooler objects.

Heat travels or is transferred from one place to another in three ways: by means of conduction, convection, or radiation.

If a warm object touches a cooler object, its heat will go directly to the cooler object by means of conduction.

If a warm object sits in cool air, its heat will go off into the cool air and will rise as warm air. Then more cool air will come in

RADIATION FROM SUN

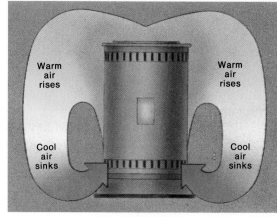

Warm air rises

Warm air rises

Cool air sinks

Cool air sinks

CONVECTION HEATER

contact with it, become
warmed, and then rise.
That is called convection.

The third way heat
travels is by radiation.
Even if a warm object is
in a vacuum, it wants to
give up its heat. It will
radiate its heat away. The
process is called radiation.

CONDUCTION

Conduction is the process of transferring heat from molecule to molecule.

Metals are better conductors of heat and electricity than wood, glass, or plastic.

Plastics are bad conductors of heat, so they make good handles for pots and pans. Bad conductors of heat are called insulators.

EXPERIMENT

Put a metal spoon and a plastic spoon in a glass of hot water. Which spoon handle warms up faster?

The metal spoon warms faster because it conducts heat better than plastic.

CONVECTION

Convection is the process of transmitting heat by means of the movement of heated matter from one place to another. It takes place in liquids and gases.

One of the main ways by which heat is passed from one place to another is by convection currents.

When a liquid or a gas is heated, the energy

In hot air balloons the heated air will expand and cause the balloon to rise. When the air inside the bag cools the balloon will fall.

passed into it causes its molecules to become excited. They move about rapidly and move farther away from each other. In other words, the substance expands.

As this happens, the substance becomes less dense. (Density indicates how close together the particles in an object are.) A gallon of warm air, therefore, weighs less than a gallon of cold air and will tend to float atop cold air. The result is, warm air rises and cold air falls.

Hang gliders (above) are built
to copy the way birds fly.

The rising warm air in
convection currents can
be used. Gliders gain
altitude on the rising
air currents caused by
convection. Eagles and
other birds glide on the
same principle.

It is easy to see how convection currents behave in a liquid.

EXPERIMENT

Put only one side of the pan over the heating element on the stove. Put some food coloring into the pan. Watch it rise on the warm side and drop on the cool side. It will continue that way in a circular motion. That is a convection cycle or convection current.

RADIATION

In both conduction and convection, heat is transmitted by moving particles. But heat can also travel where matter doesn't exist.

For example, the sun's heat reaches the earth after passing through several million miles where matter doesn't exist.

If you lie on the beach in the sun, you receive the

sun's radiation or its radiant heat. The sun is just about the earth's only source of radiation and keeps our planet warm.

Heat waves and light waves are of the same nature. Both are electromagnetic radiations. They differ only in wavelength. Heat waves are longer than light waves. Heat waves are often called infrared rays.

EXPERIMENTS

Place a black frying pan and a silver frying pan in sunlight. Which warms up first?

Take two thermometers. Place one in sunlight and the other in the shade.

The object in the sun gets warmer because heat was radiated from the sun and was carried by its light.

HEAT AND TEMPERATURE

Temperature is a measure of how hot or cold something is.

Ice is cold. It has a low temperature.

A fire is hot. It has a high temperature.

Iron and steel melt when the temperature is hot enough.

A thermometer measures how warm or hot something is. Temperature is marked in degrees.

There are two kinds of thermometers. A Fahrenheit thermometer measures in degrees Fahrenheit. A Celsius or centigrade thermometer measures in degrees centigrade.

The temperature of a body is the measure of the average kinetic energy of individual molecules. Heat is the measure of the total kinetic energy of all the molecules of the body.

How does a thermometer work?

As mercury molecules in the thermometer warm up, they vibrate more rapidly. They begin to take up more room, so they move higher up the tube. You can measure temperature by how far the mercury rises, because the molecules are bumping against each other.

The following experiment shows how this happens.

EXPERIMENT

Add some food coloring to the water inside a bottle. Put a cork or rubber stopper on the top and insert a glass tube down the neck of the bottle.

As the water heats up, it will rise in the glass tube. If you let the water cool, it will go back down the tube.

Why? As the water cools, its molecules vibrate more slowly. Thus they need less room and the water contracts or shrinks.

EXPANSION AND CONTRACTION

The hotter many things get, the larger they become. They expand.

As things get cooler, they get smaller. They contract.

The amount of expansion or contraction may not be great. You may be able to see it only with a microscope. But it is still important.

As heat energy enters

When a volcano heats up it expands. When it cools down it contracts.

a solid substance, its
atoms and molecules vibrate
vigorously. As the
vibration builds up, nearby
atoms and molecules are
pushed away from each
other faster. The space
they take up is increased,
so the solid has to expand.

Here is a way heat makes molecules move faster so things expand.

EXPERIMENT

Put water in a teakettle and heat it on a stove. When the water begins to boil, some of its molecules will move so fast that they fly out of the spout of the kettle. This is called steam. Steam will occupy more space than the water.

Steam occupies more space than water.

Here is a fun way to learn about contraction.

EXPERIMENT

Find a bottle with an opening about the size of an egg. Peel a hard-boiled egg and place it on the opening of the bottle.

Place the empty bottle in a pan of water and bring the water to a boil.

Heat will cause air inside the bottle to expand and rise.

While the water is boiling, take the bottle with the egg out of the water and set it aside.

When the bottle is cool, the air in it will cool and contract. The egg will be sucked inside the bottle!

Here are more experiments in expansion and contraction.

EXPERIMENT

Fill a balloon full of air. Do this indoors. Measure the balloon's outside circumference with a tape measure.

If it is cold outside, take the balloon outdoors. Otherwise put it in a refrigerator. The air inside the balloon will cool and the balloon will get smaller or go limp.

EXPERIMENT

Take a jar that hasn't been opened. Try to take the lid off. If the lid is stuck tightly, run some hot water over the lid. The lid will expand and you should be able to remove it easily.

Next, tighten the lid while it is still hot and put the jar in the refrigerator. Leave it there for about fifteen minutes.

Now try to take off the lid. Cooling causes contraction and the lid gets a little smaller. You may not be able to open the lid until it's put under hot water again.

You've learned what heat is, how it travels, how it converts into energy.

You discovered the ways heat makes things contract or expand.

Heat will play increasingly important roles in our future. One day, people may live and work in colonies in outer space. Their rocket ships will be launched into space because heat is converted into energy to lift the rockets.

Space may be the home for future generations.

WORDS YOU SHOULD KNOW

atom(AT • um) — the smallest bit of an element that can exist alone

conduction(kun • DUCK • shun) — serving as a channel to carry heat, electricity, sound, etc.

contraction(kun • TRACK • shun) — being made tighter or shorter

convection(kun • VEK • shun) — the transference of heat by the circulation or movement of the heated parts of a liquid or gas

energy(EN • er • jee) — the power to do work

engine(EN • jun) — a machine using the energy of steam, gasoline, or wood

expansion(ex • PAN • shun) — the act of enlarging or spreading something out

fossil fuels(FAHS • ul FYOOLS) — coal, wood, oil, and gas that evolved from ancient dead animals or plants

friction(FRICK • shun) — the rubbing of one thing against another

fuels(FYOOLS) — things that are burned to give off heat or energy

generator(JEN • er • a • ter) — a machine that makes electricity

gravity(GRAV • ih • tee) — the force by which the earth pulls objects toward its center

heat(HEET) — the quality or condition of being hot; a form of energy in the motion of molecules

kinetic energy(kuh • NET • ick EN • er • jee) — energy of motion

mercury(MUR • kur • ee) — a heavy, silver-white metallic element

molecule(MOLL • eh • kyool) — the smallest physical unit of anything

particle(PAR • tuh • kull) — a piece or bit

potential energy(puh • TEN • chull EN • er • jee) — stored-up or possible energy

radiation(ray • dee • A • shun) — the giving off and spreading out of rays of heat, light, electricity, or sound

solar(SO • ler) — of or related to the sun

temperature(TEM • per • uh • cher) — the degree of heat

thermometer(ther • MOM • uh • ter) — an instrument for measuring temperature

transfer(TRANS • fer) — to move from one place or object to another

transport(TRANS • port) — to carry or convey from one place to another

vacuum(VACK • yoom) — a space without any matter

vibration(vi • BRAY • shun) — moving or shaking rapidly

INDEX

About the author

Walter Oleksy, a Chicago area free-lance writer, is the author of forty-four books, most of them for children. A former newspaper reporter and magazine editor, Oleksy, a bachelor, lives in Evanston, Illinois, with his fourteen-year-old Labrador.

29995

536
O   Olesky, Walter

        Experiments with
        heat

$11.

536
O   Olesky, Walter

        Experiments with
        heat

$11.67

DATE	BORROWER'S NAME	
1/25/89	Nicole	
12-1-89	Mitn	124
5/11/89	Viole	128